ISAAC ASIMOV'S
Library of the Universe

The SUN

by Isaac Asimov

Gareth Stevens Publishing
Milwaukee

Library of Congress Cataloging-in-Publication Data

Asimov, Isaac, 1920-
  The sun.

  (Isaac Asimov's library of the universe)
  Bibliography: p.
  Includes index.
  Summary: Discusses the origins, physical makeup, and relationship to earth
of the huge star called the sun.
  1. Sun—Juvenile literature. [1. Sun] I. Title. II. Series: Asimov, Isaac,
1920-   . Library of the universe.
  QB521.5.A84 1988   523.7   87-42595
  ISBN 1-55532-375-8
  ISBN 1-55532-350-2 (lib. bdg.)

A Gareth Stevens Children's Books edition. Edited, designed, and produced by

Gareth Stevens, Inc.
7317 West Green Tree Road   Milwaukee, Wisconsin 53223, USA

Cover photography courtesy of NASA

Designer: Laurie Shock
Picture research: Kathy Keller
Artwork commissioning: Kathy Keller and Laurie Shock
Project editors: Mark Sachner and Rhoda Sherwood

Technical adviser and consulting editor: Greg Walz-Chojnacki

3 4 5 6 7 8 9 93 92 91 90 89 88

CONTENTS

Introduction

The Universe we live in is an enormously large place. Only in the last 50 years or so have we learned how large it really is.

It's only natural that we would want to understand the place we live in, so in the last 50 years we have developed new instruments that help us understand it. We have probes, satellites, radio telescopes, and many other things that tell us far more about the Universe than could possibly be imagined when I was young.

Nowadays, we see planets up close. We have learned about quasars and pulsars, about black holes and supernovas. We have come up with fascinating ideas about how the Universe may have come into being and how it may end. Nothing can be more astonishing and more interesting.

But of all the portions of the Universe we see in the sky, surely the most spectacular is the Sun. When it is in the sky, it drowns out everything else. It is so bright, we cannot look at it directly. In fact, we had better not try, because it can quickly damage our eyes.

When it shines, all is bright and we can see. When clouds cover it, the day turns gloomy. At night, when it is not overhead, the sky is dark. Then, unless we have artificial light, the world seems strange and dangerous. So let's learn more about our star, the Sun.

Heat! Light! Energy! The Sun supplies many of life's basic needs.
The beauty of the sunrise each morning is an extra gift.

The Birth of the Sun

How did our Sun come to be? According to scientists, about
five billion years ago, a huge cloud of dust and gas swirled in the
Universe. Perhaps a star nearby exploded, and the gases driving
out of the star pushed this cloud together. It started to contract.
Then the cloud's own gravity made it continue to contract. As
it contracted, it grew hotter and hotter. Finally, the center of
the cloud became so hot that the material in it began to change.
These changes produced still more heat. The center of the cloud
"caught fire" and became the Sun. Groups of material on the
outer rim of the cloud contracted on their own and became the
different planets in our Solar system.

© Julian Baum 1987

1. A great cloud of gas and dust in a sunless sky.

© Julian Baum 1987

2. A nearby star explodes in a stupendous supernova.

© Julian Baum 1987

3. The cloud begins to contract. Its center glows.

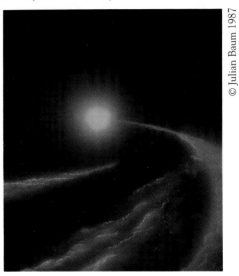

© Julian Baum 1987

4. The center heats up and the cloud flattens out.

© Julian Baum 1987

5. The center erupts, and the Sun is born!

© Julian Baum 1987

6. The planets calmly orbit the Sun as we know it today.

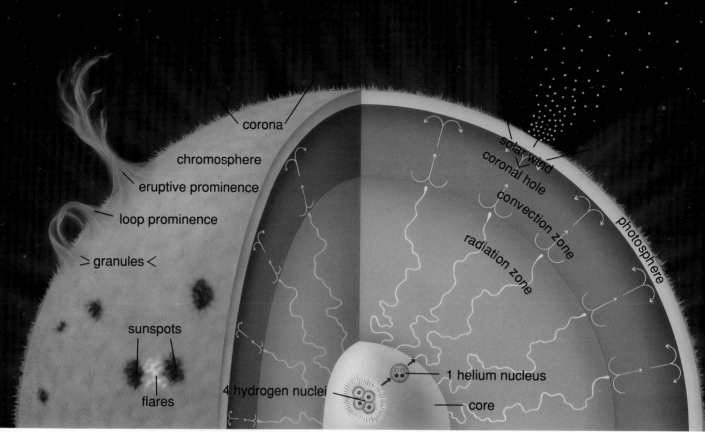

The structure of the Sun. Though gravity holds it together, the Sun has actually been exploding for billions of years. Hydrogen atoms fuse into helium, releasing energy that makes its way out of the center as light and heat.

© Lynette Cook 1987

From H-Bombs to Sunlight

What might have happened at the center of the cloud to make the Sun catch fire? To understand, let's compare the Sun to a hydrogen bomb. In a hydrogen bomb, heat develops. This forces atoms of hydrogen to smash into each other and cling together, or fuse, forming helium. This fusion produces enormous energies. Well, the Sun is about three-quarters hydrogen. The Sun's center is so hot that the hydrogen fuses into helium. This creates the energy that leaks out of the Sun's surface as light and heat. We might say the Sun is a huge hydrogen bomb that has been exploding for billions of years. Fortunately, the Sun's gravity holds it together and keeps the explosion from going out of control.

We could call the Sun a naturally occurring hydrogen bomb. Here is an unnaturally occurring hydrogen bomb — one made by humans as a weapon.

NOAO

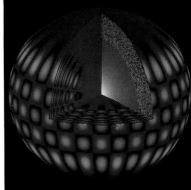

A computer made this picture to show how the Sun oscillates, or wavers. The reds show regions moving back. The blues show regions moving forward. Pictures like this help scientists learn about the structure and inside activity of the Sun.

Brookhaven National Laboratory

A neutrino detector. This instrument allows scientists to trap and count neutrinos.

The case of the missing neutrinos

When hydrogen fuses to helium deep in the Sun's center it produces certain very tiny particles called neutrinos. These are hard to detect. But in the 1970s, an American scientist, Raymond Davis, worked out a way. He tried to trap at least a few neutrinos that came from the Sun. He didn't expect many, but the number he got was only one-third the number he had expected to get! The experiment has been repeated over and over, and each time there is a neutrino shortage. Why? Do scientists have the wrong idea about what goes on inside the Sun? It's just not clear.

Ruler of the Solar System

This brilliant star is huge. It is about 93 million miles away (150 million km). So it must be huge to be seen, at that distance in the sky, as such a large ball. It is about 865,000 miles across (1,390,000 km), 108 times as wide as Earth. It has 333,400 times the mass of Earth. In fact, it has almost 1,000 times the combined mass of all the planets, satellites, asteroids, and comets circling it! The Sun's gravitational pull is so strong that it holds all those objects and forces them to move about it. Our Earth is one of those planets turning around the Sun, making one complete circle in a year.

The Sun erupting. The size of the Earth as shown in this picture gives you an idea of how huge Solar eruptions can be. If we could harness the energy from an eruption like this, we would have enough power for all human needs for the next 2,000 years. This eruption occurred on June 10, 1973, and was recorded by Skylab 2.

NASA

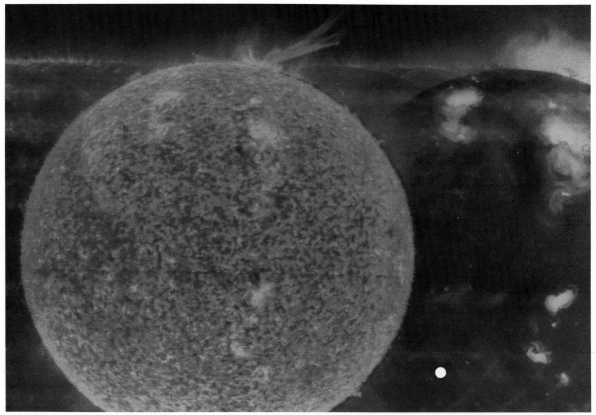

Our Earth-Moon system — peanuts to the Sun!

Here's one way to think about the Sun's size. Imagine that Earth is placed in the center of the Sun. Also imagine that the Moon is circling the Earth at its usual distance of 238,857 miles (384,321 km). The Moon, as it circled, would still be inside the Sun. In fact, it would be only a little over halfway to the Sun's surface. In other words, the Sun alone is bigger than the entire Earth-Moon system! Astronauts have traveled from Earth to the Moon, but they have not yet gone far enough to match the distance from the Sun's center to the Sun's surface.

As Earth revolves, or orbits, around the Sun, the northern and southern ends of Earth's axis take turns tilting toward the Sun. Summer comes to the hemisphere that tilts toward the Sun; winter comes to the hemisphere that tilts away from the Sun. The amount of time it takes Earth to complete its orbit is of special importance to us. We call it a year.

© Julian Baum 1987

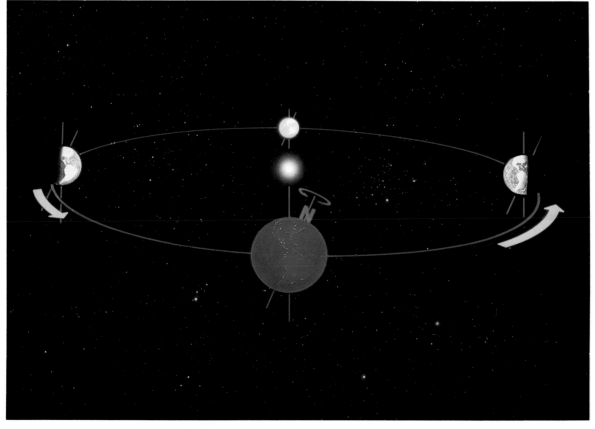

Our Star, the Sun

Why do we need this powerful star? In ancient times, at night when the Sun was not in the sky, our world was dark except for the dim light of a campfire or the Moon. It was also cold, especially in the winter and especially when the campfire burned low. How relieved people were when the Sun finally rose! Then the light came, and the Earth grew warm again.

Ra, the Sun god of ancient Egyptian mythology, was usually shown with a hawk's head on a human body. He controlled the Universe by rowing the Sun across the sky in his boat, taking the world from day to night and back to day again. Many ancient religions felt that the creation of the world was made possible by the power of the Sun and its gods.

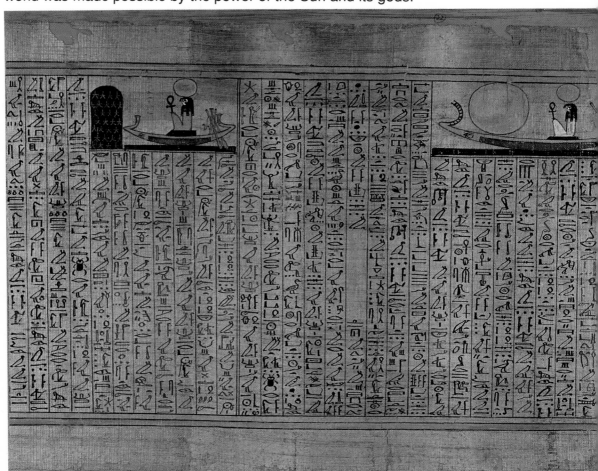

When you think about the Sun's light and warmth, it's no wonder many primitive people worshipped it as a god. They had good reason to. Without the Sun, everything would freeze, plants would not grow, animals would not have food. Without the Sun, in fact, there would be no life on Earth.

British Museum

Our Sun: not too big, not too small – just right!

The more massive a star, the shorter its lifetime. A massive star has more hydrogen to undergo fusion and produce energy. But the hydrogen in a massive star must fuse very rapidly to produce the energy to keep the star from collapsing under its own gravitational pull. An extremely massive star might survive only 100 million years. Then it would explode and collapse. That's not enough time for life to develop. A very small star, on the other hand, might last 200 billion years. But a small star wouldn't produce enough energy for life to develop. Our middle-sized star, the Sun, is just right. It not only produces enough energy for life but also will survive for a total of 10 billion years. This gives the time needed for life to form.

The swirling waves on the Sun mean that the Sun's surface rises and sinks. The wavy surface of the Sun is made up of granules that come and go like bubbles in boiling water. Each granule has about an eight-minute existence — its moment in the Sun!

The Sun's Surface: Waves of Grain

The Sun's surface is not even. Parts of it are always rising, and other parts are sinking. It's a little bit like the water of Earth's ocean that rises and falls in waves. As a result of this rising and sinking, the surface of the Sun seems to consist of grains, granules, or granulation cells of matter packed closely together. Each grain looks small to us on Earth, but on the average it is nearly 600 miles (1,000 km) across! Although large, a granule does not live long. Each lasts about eight minutes. Then a new one forms, just as bubbles keep on replacing one another in a pan of boiling water. Scientists think that there are about four million granules on the Sun's surface at any one time!

Big Bear Solar Observatory

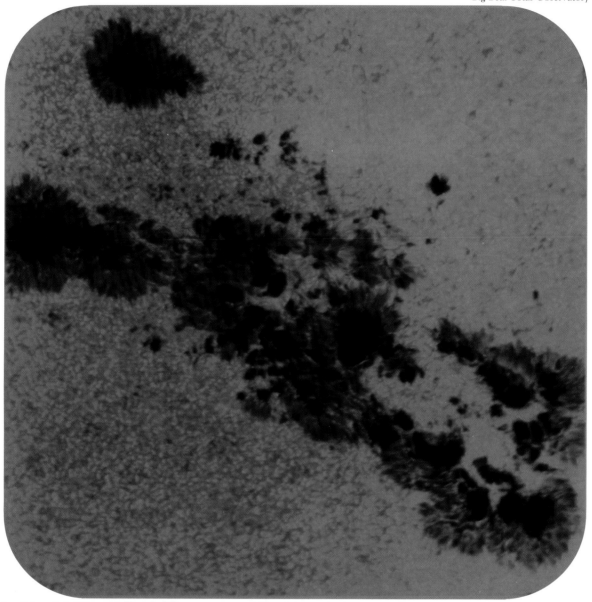

In this picture, small granules surround the large dark sunspots.
The Sun's granules may look small, but each of those "tiny"
grains averages about 600 miles (1,000 km) in diameter.

Spots and Flares

The temperature at the Sun's surface is over 10,000° F (about 5,500° C). At the center, the temperature is about 25,000,000° F (about 14,000,000° C). But this central heat leaks outward only very slowly. On the Sun's surface this heat energy is very active. Here and there, the hot gases expand and become cooler. The cooler gases shine less brightly than the hot gases do, so some areas are dark. A dark region is a sunspot. The number of sunspots on the Sun varies. Some years there are over 100 sunspots, and in some years there are fewer than 10.

In areas around sunspots, the gases are more active. Explosions near these spots give off a lot of energy. When waves from the explosions hit Earth, they even affect compasses on planes and ships! These explosions, called flares, also shine brightly. So while the sunspots are somewhat cooler — around 8,100° F (4,500° C) — the flares are hot and more than make up for sunspots. When the Sun is particularly spotty, Earth is also a bit warmer than at other times.

Images of a bipolar sunspot, recorded on February 13, 1978. A bipolar sunspot has north and south magnetic poles. Left: a magnetogram, showing the magnetic fields. Yellow indicates north; purple, south. Center: a white light photograph. Right: The yellow in this picture shows material flowing <u>away</u> from Earth out of the sunspot. Blue indicates material flowing <u>toward</u> Earth.

NOAO

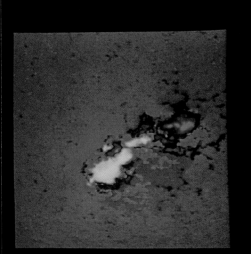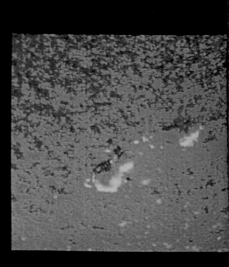

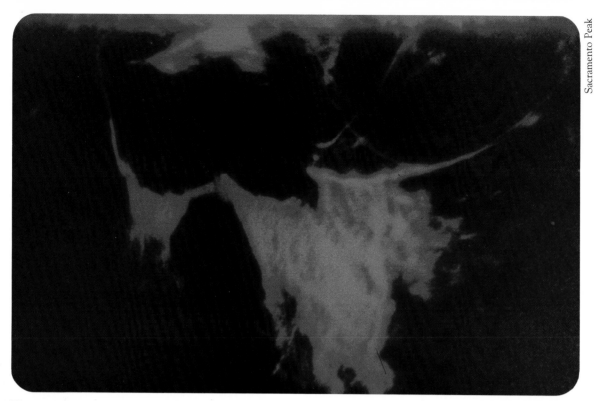

Sacramento Peak

The enormous power of Solar flares can even reach to Earth, distorting compass readings on planes and ships.

A rare spiral-shaped sunspot, February 19, 1982. Normally, sunspots are seen as irregularly shaped dark holes. This unusual sunspot had a diameter six times that of Earth!

NOAO

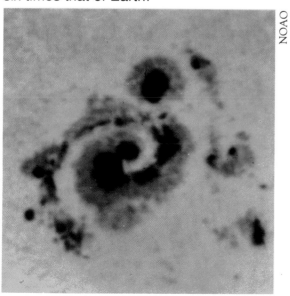

© Sally Bensusen 1987

The hotter gases on the Sun's surface shine more brightly than the cooler gases. The cooler gases form dark areas — sunspots. In this picture, the bright flashes are flares.

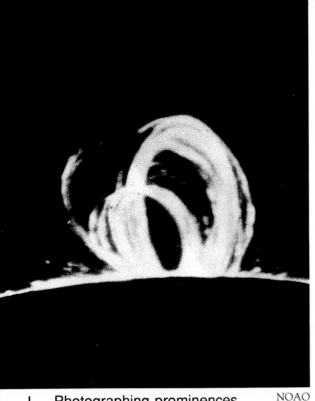

The face, or photosphere, of the Sun with prominences.

© George East

NASA

Photographing prominences requires a longer exposure than photographing the Sun itself. That is why photographers often mask out the Sun so they can record the prominence without overexposing the whole picture.

NOAO

Ribbons of Gas

Between sunspots are dark ribbons, or filaments, which are called prominences. Like sunspots, prominences are made of cooler gases. Scientists think these prominences occur just before flares become active. The prominences lift off the

The Sun's photosphere with loop prominences. The shape of loop prominences is caused by strong magnetic fields that bend the hot gases into a loop. The prominences hold hot, electrically charged gases above the Sun's active regions.

Sun's surface and erupt through its thin outer atmosphere, called the corona. The gases of the corona glow with red light and then sink down to the surface of the Sun. We can see these ribbons of gas with special instruments. When looked at straight on, these ribbons look like dark filaments. But coming off the edge of the Sun, they form graceful arches, tens of thousands of miles high.

The longest spike, or streamer, in this picture projects more than one million miles (1.61 million km) beyond the Sun's surface. Just after this coronagraph was taken, a Solar flare erupted on the right edge of the Sun. Within minutes the corona changed its shape.

Does the Sun influence the Earth?

Does the Sun influence the Earth? Of course it does. It gives us light and warmth. But what about the sunspot cycle? Every 11 years, the Sun gets very spotty at sunspot maximum and almost clear at sunspot minimum. That means the Sun gets a trifle warmer and then a trifle cooler. Does this affect Earth's temperature, its harvests, its rainfall? Possibly. Some people even think that the sunspot cycle might affect stock market prices, the ups and downs of the economy, and so on. It seems hard to believe – but is it possible?

Skylab took this coronagraph of the Sun in 1974. That day the emissions beyond the Sun's corona extended for millions of miles.

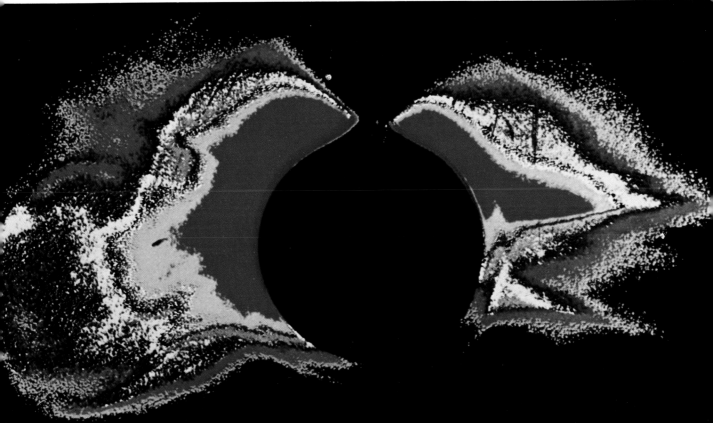

The aurora is a common sight over Canada or Alaska. But this picture is unusual because it was taken in Arizona, where the sight of the aurora is quite rare. Shown here beneath the aurora is the Kitt Peak National Observatory.

The Sunlight of Night

All this activity on the Sun's surface sends tiny particles outward in all directions. These particles carry electric charges and travel at a speed of about 300 miles (500 km) a second. This stream of particles is called the solar wind.

This wind reaches far out in space, passing by the various planets. When it reaches Earth, it strikes the upper atmosphere, particularly near the North and South Poles. The energy from this collision then releases energy in the form of light. As a result, the polar nights are lit by faint-colored light in streamers and curves. This light is called the aurora. Sometimes, when the Sun is very active, the aurora can be seen beyond the polar regions.

Two photos of the Aurora Borealis, or Northern Lights, over Alaska. The aurora that is visible in the southern hemisphere is called Aurora Australis.

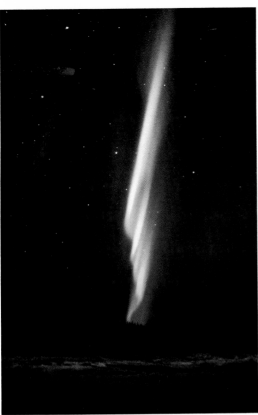

© Forrest Baldwin

© Forrest Baldwin

© Mark Paternostro 1988

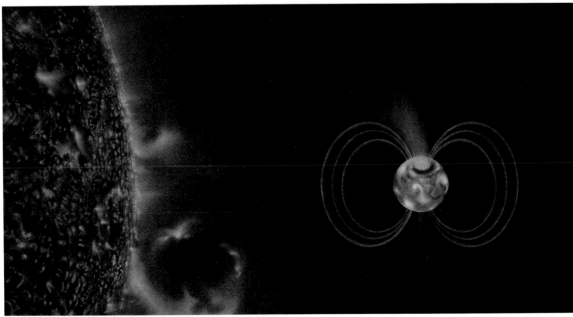

An illustration showing the Sun and Earth's magnetosphere. The magnetosphere shields Earth from the solar wind. But, as the picture shows, it also allows the solar wind into the upper atmosphere over the North and South Poles.

Daytime Night

Our Moon has helped us learn about the Sun — without our even leaving Earth. Sometimes the Sun seems to grow dark in the middle of a cloudless sky. This is because the Moon sometimes moves directly between us and the Sun. The Moon can sometimes block the entire body of the Sun. But the Sun's corona shines softly as a kind of halo around the Moon. This blocking is a total solar eclipse. It can last up to seven and a half minutes, at the most, before part of the Sun shows again. Each year there are from two to five partial eclipses. Since the Moon's shadow falls over only a small part of Earth in one eclipse, people in any one area on Earth see a total solar eclipse only about once every 300 years.

NASA

A 1970 solar eclipse passes by a tracking station at Wallops Island, Virginia.

© Richard Hill

A partial eclipse of the Sun: The Moon is moving across the Sun's face.

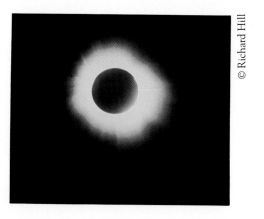

© Richard Hill

A total eclipse of the Sun: Only the Sun's corona is visible.

During a total eclipse of the Sun, the Moon blocks out the Sun's light from part of Earth. Within the smallest circle in this picture, the sky would be quite dark and a person's view of the Sun would be that of the total eclipse. People within the outer circle would find daylight to be a strange kind of shadow and the Sun only partially eclipsed by the Moon.

NOAO

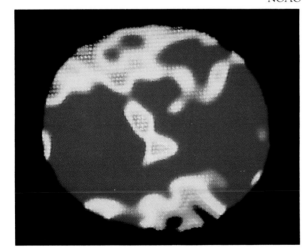

Many photographic images were taken and combined to produce this single computer-generated image of the giant Betelgeuse.

The red giants — big, bigger, biggest

As large as the Sun is, it is not the largest star. There are stars called red giants that are so huge they stretch across four or five hundred million miles (six or eight hundred million km). Imagine that the Sun was in the center of a red giant — such as the one named Betelgeuse. That red giant would stretch out past the Earth and maybe even past Mars! Of course, red giant stars have their material spread out very thinly. But even so, Betelgeuse is 18 times as massive as the Sun. There are other stars that are 90 to 100 times as massive as the Sun.

New Ways to View the Sun

Most of the time, we use instruments to study the Sun. Since 1814, an instrument called the spectroscope has been used to watch sunlight. It spreads out, in order of length, the tiny waves that make up light. Different wavelengths have different colors. Beginning in 1891, scientists used an instrument called a spectroheliograph to study the Sun by examining a particular wavelength. This helped tell them what elements made up the Sun. And since 1931, we haven't had to wait for an eclipse to look directly at the Sun. Since then, even when there is no eclipse, scientists have used the coronagraph to cover the Sun and study the corona.

NOAO

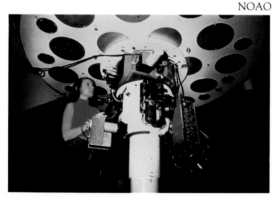

An astronomer at Kitt Peak examines a spectroheliograph attached to a telescope.

NOAO

Navajo students examine a Solar image in the McMath Solar Telescope at Kitt Peak. The McMath gives the largest, clearest image of our Sun.

A sunspot shot taken at Kitt Peak. On the right, a white, or natural, light shot of the sunspot. On the left, a spectrum shot of the same area.

NOAO

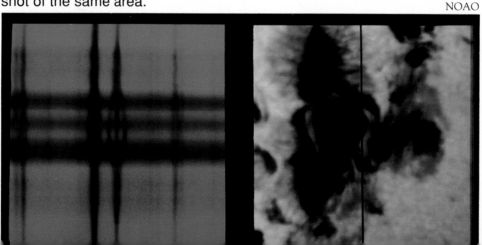

Solar spectrum: The visible or white light portion of the spectrum of the
Sun has been split into all its colors in this spectrogram.

Rainbow — a naturally occurring spectrogram!

Skylab 3: This view of Skylab in Earth orbit was taken from the Command/Service Module during a "fly around" inspection of the orbiting satellite. Earth's clouds and water are visible far below.

The Sun from Space

Other tools help us see the Sun from outside our atmosphere. Not all the radiation from the Sun reaches the Earth. The atmosphere absorbs much of the radiation before it can reach us. So there is a lot about the Sun that we cannot know from Earth.

In order to study all the radiation from the Sun, we must observe it from space, from outside the atmosphere. Special satellites have been used for such studies since 1957. Many nations have built and launched these satellites, including the US, the Soviet Union, Japan, West Germany, and India. In 1973, a satellite named Skylab carried human beings into space, where they could study the Sun's radiation. They also discovered some regions in the corona that were cool and had little gas in them. These regions are called coronal holes.

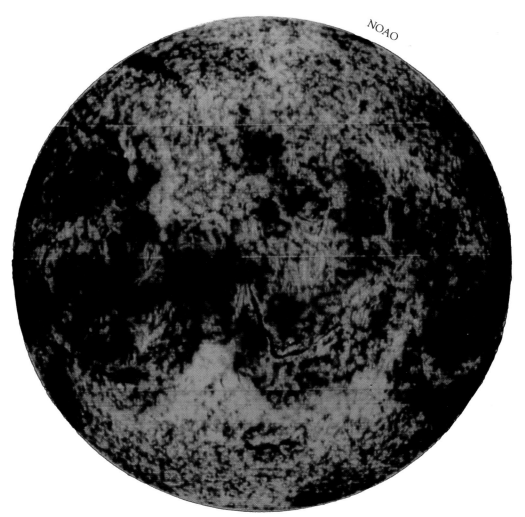

This ultraviolet picture of the Sun shows a coronal
hole in the Sun's outer atmosphere. Coronal holes
are believed to be the main outlet for the solar wind.

Probing the Sun's Secrets

There is still a great deal to find out about the Sun and how we can use it creatively on Earth. Scientists, for instance, continue to study the sunspot cycle — the rise and fall in the number of sunspots from year to year. If they learn why it takes place, they may learn more about what goes on deep inside the Sun.

We have learned how to harness some of the Sun's energy for heating. Many buildings have special devices that capture the Sun's rays and store their heat for later use. These devices help us conserve resources like coal and oil that are running out. Who knows what we might be able to do someday as we continue to unravel the mysteries of our star, the Sun?

Star Probe — a possible addition to Earth's fleet of space probes. It would send back new pictures and information about our star. NASA

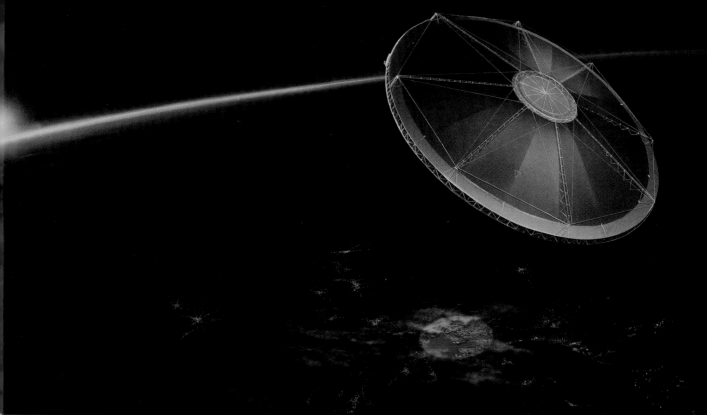

Light in an emergency: Why should nightfall keep the Sun from lighting up our lives? A huge Space Mirror satellite could reflect the Sun's light at night, providing light during a blackout. In this illustration, blacked-out New York City is the lucky recipient of emergency sunlight.

The case of the missing sunspots

It seems the sunspot cycle isn't always with us. The Italian scientist Galileo discovered sunspots in 1610. Others observed them, too. But then, between 1645 and 1715, hardly a sunspot was to be seen on the Sun. After that, the familiar sunspot cycle began. We call the spotless period between 1645 and 1715 a Maunder minimum, because an astronomer named Maunder discussed it in 1890. Apparently, there have been similar periods when sunspots were missing throughout history. What causes the cycle to suddenly stop and then restart? Right now, astronomers aren't sure.

Fact File: The Sun

The Sun is, of course, our very own star. As far as stars go, the Sun is not all that big. But its diameter is about 108 times bigger than that of Earth. And it is about 270,000 times closer to Earth than is Alpha Centauri, the next closest star. So it looks quite big to us here on Earth. While the light from Alpha Centauri takes over four years to reach Earth, the light from the Sun takes only about eight minutes. So, though the Sun is small compared to many stars, its size and distance from Earth have combined to sustain life on our planet very nicely.

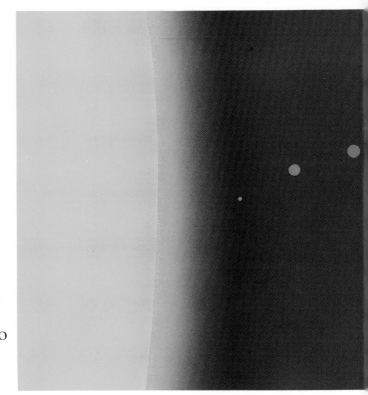

Here is a close-up of the Sun and some of its special features, as well as some fascinating comparisons between our star and our planet, Earth.

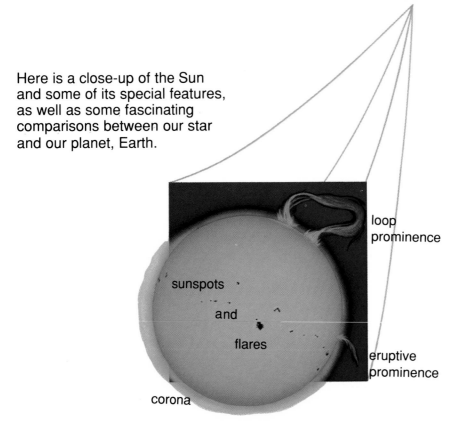

loop prominence

sunspots

and

flares

eruptive prominence

corona

Object	Diameter
Sun	864,988 miles (1,392,000 km)
Earth	7,927 miles (12,756 km)

The Sun and Its Family of Planets

The Sun and its Solar system family, left to right: Mercury, Venus, Earth, Mars, Jupiter, Saturn, Uranus, Neptune, Pluto.

© Sally Bensusen 1987

The Sun: How It Measures Up				
Rotation Period (length of day)	**Period of Orbit Around Sun (length of year)**	**Surface Gravity**	**Distance from Sun (nearest-farthest)**	**Least Time It Takes for Light to Travel to Earth**
25-35 days	—	27.9*	—	8.3 minutes
23 hours, 56 minutes	365.25 days (one year)	1.00*	91-95 million miles (147-152 million km)	—

* Multiply your weight by this number to find out how much you would weigh on the Sun or Earth.

More Books About the Sun

Here are more books that contain information about the Sun and its neighborhood, the Solar system. If you are interested in them, check your library or bookstore.

Done in the Sun: Solar Projects for Children. Hillerman (Sunstone)
How Did We Find Out about Solar Power? Asimov (Avon)
Our Solar System. Asimov (Gareth Stevens)
Space Trip! Couper (Gareth Stevens)
The Sun. Petty (Franklin Watts)
Sun and Stars. Barrett (Franklin Watts)
Sun Calendar. Jacobs (Silver Burdett)

Places to Visit

You can explore the Universe — including the Sun and our Solar system — without leaving Earth. Here are some museums and centers where you can find many different kinds of space exhibits.

NASA Goddard Space Flight Center
Greenbelt, Maryland

National Air and Space Museum
Smithsonian Institution
Washington, DC

Astrocentre
Royal Ontario Museum
Toronto, Ontario

Lawrence Hall of Science
Berkeley, California

Kansas Cosmosphere and Space Center
Hutchinson, Kansas

The Space and Rocket Center
Huntsville, Alabama

For More Information About the Sun

Here are some people you can write to for more information about the Sun. Be sure to tell them exactly what you want to know about. And include your age, full name, and address so they can write back to you.

For information about the Sun:
STARDATE
MacDonald Observatory
Austin, Texas 78712

NASA Jet Propulsion Laboratory
Public Affairs 180-201
4800 Oak Grove Drive
Pasadena, California 91109

About space energy:
NASA Lewis Research Center
Educational Services Office
21000 Brookpark Road
Cleveland, Ohio 44135

For astro-photography of the Sun:
Caltech Bookstore
California Institute of Technology
Mail Code 1-51
Pasadena, California 91125

Glossary

asteroids: very small planets made of rock or metal. There are thousands of them in our Solar system, and they mainly orbit the Sun between Mars and Jupiter. Some show up elsewhere in the Solar system, however — some as meteoroids. Many scientists feel that the two moons of Mars are actually "captured" asteroids.

aurora: light at the North and South Poles caused by the collision of the solar wind with our outer atmosphere.

corona: the thin outer atmosphere of the Sun.

flares: explosions near sunspots that give off great energy.

fusion: the coming together of hydrogen atoms. This produces enormous energy.

granule: one of the cell-like spots on the Sun's surface that disappear after a brief time, usually about eight minutes. An average granule is about 600 miles (1,000 km) across.

gravity: the force that causes objects like the Sun and its planets to be attracted to one another.

helium: a gas formed in the Sun by the fusion of hydrogen atoms.

hydrogen: a colorless, odorless gas that is the simplest and lightest of the elements. The Sun is about three-quarters hydrogen.

neutrinos: very tiny particles produced when hydrogen fuses to helium in the center of the Sun.

prominences: dark ribbons between sunspots that may occur just before flares become active.

radio telescope: an instrument that uses a radio receiver and antenna to both see into space and listen for messages from space.

red giants: huge stars that may be 400 million miles (640 million km) across.

Skylab: a satellite carrying humans launched in 1973.

Solar system: the Sun with the planets and all the other bodies, such as the asteroids, that orbit the Sun.

solar wind: tiny particles that travel from the Sun's surface at a speed of 300 miles (500 km) a second.

spectroscope, spectroheliograph, and coronagraph: devices used by scientists to study the Sun.

Sun: our star and provider of the energy that makes life possible on Earth.

sunspot: a dark area on the Sun caused by gases that are cooler and shine less brightly than hot gases.

total solar eclipse: the blocking of the entire body of the Sun by the Moon.

Index

The publishers wish to thank the following for permission to reproduce copyright material: front cover, pp. 8, 16 (lower), 17 (both), 20 (upper right), 24, 26, courtesy of NASA; pp. 4, 16 (upper right), © George East; pp. 5 (all), 9, © Julian Baum 1987; p. 6, © Lynette Cook 1987; pp. 7 (upper right), 14, 15 (lower left), 16 (upper left), 18, 21 (lower), 22 (all), 23 (upper), 25, National Optical Astronomy Observatories; p. 7 (upper left), Defense Nuclear Agency; p. 7 (lower), Brookhaven National Laboratory; pp. 10-11, British Museum, Michael Holford Photographs; pp. 12, 13, Big Bear Solar Observatory; p. 15 (upper), Sacramento Peak Solar Observatory; pp. 15 (lower right), 21 (upper), 28-29, © Sally Bensusen 1987; p. 19 (both upper), © Forrest Baldwin; p. 20 (upper left & lower right), © Richard Hill; p. 19 (lower), © Mark Paternostro 1987; p. 23 (lower), © James Peterson; p. 27, © Mark Maxwell 1987.